The Lines

Eisha Dileep

INDIA · SINGAPORE · MALAYSIA

Copyright © Eisha Dileep 2024
All Rights Reserved.

ISBN 979-8-89588-621-2

This book has been published with all efforts taken to make the material error-free after the consent of the author. However, the author and the publisher do not assume and hereby disclaim any liability to any party for any loss, damage, or disruption caused by errors or omissions, whether such errors or omissions result from negligence, accident, or any other cause.

While every effort has been made to avoid any mistake or omission, this publication is being sold on the condition and understanding that neither the author nor the publishers or printers would be liable in any manner to any person by reason of any mistake or omission in this publication or for any action taken or omitted to be taken or advice rendered or accepted on the basis of this work. For any defect in printing or binding the publishers will be liable only to replace the defective copy by another copy of this work then available.

*To the little girl who scribbled stories in the
margins of her notebooks;
to my loved ones, the heartbeats of my life;
to those who look for comfort in verses,
may you always feel seen in these pages.*

Table of Contents

Author's Note   7

Chapter 1	For the Scars	9
Chapter 2	For Absence	19
Chapter 3	For Days of Grief	29
Chapter 4	For When You Are Healing	41
Chapter 5	For Words of Comfort	59
Chapter 6	For the Path to Growing Up	71
Chapter 7	For the Echoes of Love	85

Acknowledgments   97

About the Author   101

Author's Note

Dear Reader,

Thank you for holding this piece of my heart in your hands.

This collection of poems is a journey through the landscapes of love, loss, growth, and healing—a map of the human experience charted through verse.

These words were born from late nights and early mornings, from moments of joy and depths of sorrow. They are the whispers of my soul, the echoes of experiences both uniquely mine and universally human.

As you turn these pages, I hope you find a home in these words. May you discover a poem that speaks to your heart and gives voice to feelings you've struggled to express. Whether you're navigating the scars of love, the pain of absence, or the complexities of growing up, know that you're not alone.

Poetry has always been my refuge, my way of making sense of the world. It's been my dream since childhood to share these words with you. If even one poem resonates with you and brings you comfort or helps you feel understood, then this book has fulfilled its purpose.

Thank you for allowing my words to be a part of your journey. May you find solace, understanding, and perhaps even a reflection of yourself within these pages.

With love and hope,
Eisha Dileep.

CHAPTER 1

For the Scars

Soulfire

I don't care if you are fire,
a raging tempest, or death itself.
Suddenly, my skin is meant to burn;
my heart is meant to sink;
my life is poised to end.

If I get to feel your embrace,
pain dissolves in your tender space.
It slips away like shadows at dawn,
a bittersweet lullaby, where I'm reborn.

In that fleeting moment, I'd trade it all.
Be it the warmth of the sun,
or the light of the fall.
For just one heartbeat shared with you,
I'd surrender the world and everything I knew.

In your gaze, I find my worth,
lost in the chaos, you're my rebirth.
Even if it means losing my way,
I'd choose you in darkness, come what may.

Caged

I yearn for the spirit I once knew,
untouched by your presence.

Perhaps I was lost, but I roamed free.
I wandered wild, in sheer delight,
with every heartbeat, my spirit at ease.

Now I am trapped in this cage of attachment,
but the blame is on me for ever handing you the key.

Your shadow has fallen, turning my skies grey.
What felt like love has led me astray.
Whispers, once sweet, now echo with doubt.
In your embrace, I lost my way out.

If I could reclaim the lost parts of me,
I'd shatter these chains and rise to be free.

Yet here I stand, still caught in the snare,
yearning for the heart I once knew—
the wild, unbroken spirit that dared.

I Miss You

I miss you.
Not the version that makes me doubt myself,
but the you who listened to every word I said.

You became my home within days,
not the kind that brings peace,
but a broken home I can't quite escape.

Still, even in the cracks,
there's a trace of love that lingers.
It's not enough to fill the emptiness,
but just enough to keep me here,
caught in the echo of what we were.

So, I stay.

I stay for those moments we shared,
and the warmth that still haunts this space.
I stay to hold on to the fragments of us,
even when it hurts to remember your face.

Capricious

One day, I'm your favourite,
the sun in your sky,
and the next, we're like strangers,
as if time slipped by.

It's a dance of uncertainty,
where love fades to grey.
Each smile feels like a puzzle,
each word a game we play.

Yet here I am,
a sucker for this fight,
grasping at the shadows,
yearning for your light.

Never Enough

Why was I never enough?
I moved mountains for you,
apologised for every mistake that wasn't mine,
and bore the weight of unspoken pain.

You were the sun, and I was the earth,
revolving around you day after day,
seeking a hint of your warmth.
But I was merely a shadow, fading in your glow.

Love is built on give and take,
yet you were always the one to forsake.

Now I stand, searching for answers in the echo of what could have been.
In this battlefield of devotion and despair,
I wonder if I was ever truly seen.

From the Depths of Despair

I don't care if you rip my heart into shreds again.
At least then,
I will be reminded that I still have a heart worthy to be held,
even if it is with hands made of thorns.

I don't care if you ignite a fire that leaves me in ashes.
At least then,
I will get to feel the warmth I have been shivering for.

How?

I have accepted that our bond lies in its grave now;
we dug it together, after all.

And I know it is pointless to write about our memories,
because they will always leave a bitter aftertaste.

But how can I let go of the future we had built,
the plans we devised, the promises we swore to keep?
How can I sit in class with your desk
no longer attached to mine?
How can I move into an empty home that
our hearts were meant to occupy?
How do I replace you with people
who are too distant to understand my mind?

I can let go of you,
and I can accept that our souls will never unite,
but how can I forget about the love that was meant to be mine?

Familiar Strangers

We were once strangers, mere whispers in the crowd,
our paths uncharted, our love yet to be claimed.
If only it had lingered in that untouched space.

Now, we stand as foreigners to one another once more,
each glance a distant echo of what used to be.

It's hard to fathom how my soul finds solace in a stranger,
but then I remember—
we are only strangers by name,
never by heart.

CHAPTER 2

For Absence

Love Lingers

There are people I no longer talk to,
but I still remember the little things—
the way their laugh filled a room, the coffee shop they swore by.
A random song on the radio takes me back,
not just to them, but to who we were,
when our lives were still intertwined.

But where do I keep these bits of time?
Is there a diary that knows no end,
one that can hold the weight of enough ink
to pen down everything I remember about someone I no longer know?

Though our paths have grown apart, an imprint remains.
And even when life has shifted in colours,
I still sit under the warmth of the sun sometimes,
reminding myself of the love that once existed;
a hue I will forever carry.

The Space Between Us

The night sky we once lay beneath has now become your home.
Beneath the celestial veil we once adored,
every star was a witness to the dreams we explored.
Now, they only flicker with echoes of you.

I remember the nights when time stood still,
as we traced patterns of galaxies far.
But these days, the cosmos feels vast and cold,
your absence a shadow that darkens my nights.
The moon hangs heavy with the stories untold,
while I search for your warmth in the pale silver light.

Here I stand, feeling lost and impaired,
as the universe spins on, indifferent to my pain.

I feel sore every time I think about the stars–
once our favourite vista.
For these same little lights have wrapped you in their warmth,
far far away from me, like a dream out of reach.

The Weight of Memory

There is a weight that comes with remembering everything you have ever loved.

Every scrap brings home ghosts to a corner of my brain.
Each memory is a tear in the fabric of my soul.
All the traces of love have cemented their mark on my heart.

I cannot go back, for there is no one there,
only echoes that linger in empty rooms.
Yet I hesitate to move forward,
for the future feels like a vast unknown,
a blank canvas where I fear no one will appear.

I am caught between what I have lost
and what I am destined to lose,
trapped in the middle, holding sorrow's hand.

The Doorway

I used to wait for you by the door,
hoping you'd walk in, just once more—
with donuts in hand and flowers in bloom.
I would glance at the clock's dancing arms,
each second a reminder of wasted patience,
each tick a pulse of quiet despair.

But the doorway always stood bare—
even your shadow wouldn't come near.

Now, my time is no longer pledged to you;
the house hums with new laughter and fresh donuts.

But sometimes, I find myself drawn back to that door frame.
A fleeting thought lingers in a corner of my brain I swore to erase,
and it tries to whisper, but I can hear it trying to scream…
"What if?"

And there it waits, hovering like a ghost I refuse to see.
No matter how much life fills these walls,
the door still seems to feel ajar,
holding a silence so thick I can almost hear it breathe.

Faded Souvenirs

Your memories are slowly fading away from my life.

I remember your face,
but your sweet scent has drifted like smoke,
a fleeting whisper on the edge of my mind.
I can no longer recall the warmth of your touch,
yet I know, without question,
there's nothing that could ever compare.
The sound of your voice now blurs in my head,
but I will never forget how it was—and always will be—
my favourite sound in the world.

I feel selfish; my heart, swallowed by the void of your absence,
lost sight of the pieces of you that remain.
Caught between the ache of loss and the fear of forgetting,
I am left to mourn both your absence and the parts of you I let fade.

Hollow Home

I want to pick up your call,
to answer all the words we've left unsaid.
I want to run home to you,
to the warmth I once knew.

But you're no longer ***home***;
you've become just a house,
made of bricks and stone,
where silence fills the space that once held your voice.

I stand at the door, but the key no longer fits;
what was once familiar now feels distant,
as if love itself has shifted,
and you—once my refuge—
are just walls, cold and indifferent.

I still want to run back to you,
but now, as I reach for my phone,
a silent reminder echoes back at me.
You're just a memory wrapped in shadows of what used to be.
You're no longer my sanctuary.

Circles

I despise the winter's snow,
once your favourite shade of white,
now it drapes the world in a shroud of longing.

The autumn breeze against my skin ignites a fire,
for your hair used to dance so perfectly in tune with it.

Spring, once a canvas of joy,
feels hollow and mute.
And summer, stripped of its warmth,
no longer holds the promise of seeing you.

I hate that every part of life circles back to you,
a bittersweet ache that colours my days.

You are no longer a part of this world,
yet your shadow clings to my every breath.

It haunts the corners of my memory,
reminding me that love is an indelible stain,
one that time cannot wash away.

Lost Versions

"We're still the same," you always told me.
So why do you become a new person every time we speak?
Why do you tell me you miss me with a tone
dripping in honey, coated in excitement you reserve for your new friends?

You have outgrown the only version of you I knew,
and my heart aches with the pain of discovering the new you.

Each laughter rings foreign, a melody I can't trace,
moments we once held dear are
now tinged with a bittersweet aftertaste.

What happened to the comfort of silence shared?
Now every pause stretches like an endless night,
filled with the weight of unsaid words, so layered,
as I sift through memories, seeking the light.

I guess I must live with the truth,
that we are not the same as we used to be,
even though that is the fallacy you've been forcing me to believe.

CHAPTER 3

For Days of Grief

Love & Chaos

I was born amidst chaos.
My house was not made of feathers and fragile ceramic plates;
it did not have walls painted with floral motifs and bright spring colours.
Instead, it stood firm, where the air thickly smothers.

My house did not wrap false hope in blankets of lies,
it was the kind that taught me the cruelty of life.
I learned how to fend for myself, to be tough
and to fight through challenges, no matter how rough.

But amidst the noise and chaos,
there was no room for love that was soft and poised;
there was only place for love that was fierce—
sometimes too much, and sometimes just not enough.

Though I am glad I can be rough in a world full of strife,
there are days I long for a soft and sweet love in my life.
A love that blossoms under the sun,
that reassures me when my spirit feels weak.

But there is a fear that grips my soul,
a fear of loving too hard, of breaking something fragile and leaving it scarred.
What if I ruin this love I yearn for, like a tide raging over sandcastles?

So I remain in this shell, with my heart tightly bricked,
longing for warmth, but far too afraid to take the risk.

The Memory Keeper

To be the one who remembers is to be the one who suffers.
It is to be haunted by the ghosts of yesterday.
It is to carry a quiet ache,
a heart heavy with faces that no longer fill the room.

In this solitude, I feel the sting of absence,
the bittersweet taste of love turned to memory.
I mourn not just for what is gone,
but for the warmth of familiarity that has grown cold,
and for the stories that were left untold.

To be the one who remembers is to be the one who suffers,
but it is also to be the one who keeps alive
the love that time cannot erase.
It is to be the one who nurtures
a flickering flame that never dies.

The Last Bit of Everything

They say the best part of a book is the ending,
the most thrilling episode of a show is the finale,
and that everything will work out in the end.

But how am I meant to finish a book
if my pen is out of ink?
How can I watch the finale
if every single member of the cast has vanished?
How can I look forward to the end
when I'm not sure whether I will make it that far?

After every bad day, we are told the sun will rise again.
No matter the circumstances,
the light of day will shine upon you.

But what if I leave before dawn,
in the twilight of the morning?
What if the sun's blazing beams fail to warm my skin,
and only ghosts linger where my essence had been?

Threads of Regret

Why does regret refuse to leave my side?
Why does it echo the sounds of everything I have ever loved
amidst the walls I no longer belong?
It reminds me of all the dreams that exist
only as shards of broken hopes.

It drowns me in the pool of reminiscing,
and it does not offer me a helping hand
when I beg to be saved.
It laughs when I long for the warmth from my past,
because that has been dissolved
in the cold, barren land that now stands.

Regret watches as I sift through the embers
of a life unlived, swallowed by the endless night,
where the faint echoes now fade to silence,
and the laughter turns to dust.
It is a reminder of what might have been,
what I can never mend.

Regret drags me to this desolate landscape,
where I will wander helplessly until the end.

The Burning House

I finally escaped the burning house.
I finally have the freedom my once childish heart craved.
No more deafening nights or broken glass shards in the kitchen.

But as I drive back to the plot that holds my blazing home,
why does it stand, untouched by the flames?
Why does laughter echo from its walls?

No ashes are lying in the corners;
the blood from the bathroom floor has vanished,
wiped away like a haunting whisper that never dared to linger.

As I peek through the windows,
all I can see are picture-perfect smiles
and perfectly polished counters.
My garden is now home to blooming lilies
instead of the twisted remains of dead oak trees.

And all this only plants one seed in my head:
was I the matchstick?
Was I the reason everyone suffocated?
Maybe it wasn't the house that was engulfed in flames,
but rather the shadows within me that sparked the blaze.

The Twist of Fate

I thought the never-ending spiral
of turning lost love stories into poetry had finally ceased.
I thought the heavy feeling in my chest
would no longer weigh me down; perhaps it was finally at ease.

I thought the lump at the back of my throat
had been swallowed forever, a similar feeling nowhere to be found.
I thought the gift of healing was finally making its way to me,
slowly but steadily, like a turtle running a marathon.

But then, everything drowned.
The heavy feeling jammed up my lungs,
every breath followed by the hiccup of reality.
The lump in my throat crept back up,
ready to remind me that it was all merely a fantasy.

The love stories faded into bitter tales of distant acquaintances,
and my favourite moments were suddenly vintage.
Just when I thought I had it all,
the universe pulled the strings of my fall.

Silent Pleas

I still remember that night;
they brought you in, hands trembling for the final farewell.
Our eyes met, yours vacant, mine flooded with grief.

"Say goodbye one last time."
The words so faint, drowned in the silence that echoed.

Rose petals scattered around you, a delicate display,
their softness a cruel contrast to the pain I carried.
Within my heart, their thorns lay concealed.

Desperation's grip was suffocating, its echo a chill,
so I pleaded—
I begged God with every breath left in me,
"Take me instead," my heart's desperate will.

But the heavens remained silent, cold.
No flicker of hope stirred the void you left behind,
only the weight of absence, heavy and bold,
like a dark shadow that refused to unwind.

I reached out, fingers trembling,
but grasped only the empty chill of the night—
a harsh reminder that you were irrevocably lost.

How could the world keep turning,
when mine lay shattered, dim and burning?
Each second stretched into an aching sigh,
passing like a shadow, whispering goodbye.

Still, when I call out for you,
my whispers are swallowed by the night's heavy veil,
searching for traces of you in the silence that prevails.

The Background Friend

I know to put my footsteps behind
when there are already plenty occupying the sidewalk;
I know that when everyone wants a group picture,
I belong behind the camera.

You share your heart with me through the night,
but come dawn, your eyes turn to the light,
blinded by the brightness, you forget my name.

But I will always wait—
wait on the phone as you text back everyone but me,
wait till it is finally my turn to be your friend again,
wait till my breath runs out.

But promise me that my wait will one day be over.

Because all I want is to cross your mind,
even if it's just for a second or two.
So I can be sure I'm more than a whisper,
and not just a ghost drifting through.

Sadness' Embrace

I don't think I will ever fully shed this sadness.
I'm not saying there are no moments of joy in this life of mine,
but it seems as if embracing them is a crime.
Like a butterfly, they flutter away within seconds,
and I am too busy fearing them to enjoy their presence.

It's like comfort food—
you may try to enjoy other things,
but nothing appeals to the heart like that one meal.

It's not happiness that I fear, though.
It's the unpredictability that makes me cautious.
What if all of it is just the starter to a main course of unexpected melancholy?
Almost as if life is fooling me into believing it is no longer uncanny.

So perhaps I will always carry a hint of sadness,
not because my life is drenched in gloom,
but because it's a comfort I've always known.
It almost feels like home.

The Veil of Privilege

When I look at life through their eyes,
the sleepless nights spent over homework seem rather peaceful
compared to theirs,
spent under the cold embrace of the night sky.

When their eyes swell with tears
and their stomachs ache with hunger,
even the glimpse of the food on my plate fills me for days.
My prayers for wants feel like childish pleas,
while whispers of mothers begging for peace fill the air.

The textbooks stacked on my shelf
feel like a reminder to myself
of where fortune can be found,
for in their world, no lessons lie—just survival's constant test.

While I complain to God in the comfort of my bedroom,
there are those thanking him
for merely surviving another day.

As I wish for my dreams to come true,
I do not realise I am living someone else's.
It is a privilege to be shielded by the flimsy barrier of a screen,
where fear and horror are only a result of empathy and not our daily reality.

CHAPTER 4

For When You Are Healing

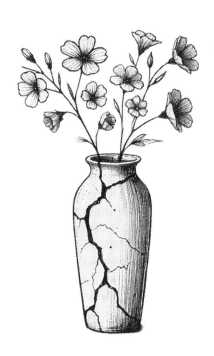

Healing Through the Looking Glass

Everyone talks about the freedom and serenity that follow healing,
but no one prepares you for the grief that trails along.

I believe that when you heal,
you are given a mirror.

Not a mirror that reflects your progress,
but one that reveals all that you have gone through,
all that you missed out on.
You see how you have been treated
and the scars your journey has etched into your skin.

Your past self is often on the other side of this mirror,
wishing you had not taken this long to heal,
to stop begging for commitment,
for closure.

Healing is not just about letting your soul free
or moving past everything that once haunted you.
Healing is about appreciating yourself
for carrying every burden you shouldn't have
and forgiving yourself for taking so long to let go of the weight.

Healing isn't just about putting a bandage on your heart,
but also swallowing the stinging sensation of cleaning the wounds it has borne.

The Butterflies

I don't look for the butterflies of love anymore;
they only bring home bundles of anxiety,
of doubt, of ambivalence.

My stomach doesn't like the jittery feeling,
and my heart desires to keep its sanity.
I do not want someone who feels like a party,
but rather the soft mattress I fall into after my worst days.

I want to feel safe and loved within their proximity.
The kind of bond where silence speaks volumes,
where no one goes to sleep with emptiness in their soul.

Therefore, my heart no longer asks for a sea of butterflies.
It only hopes for waves of serenity.

Stardust Dreams

I don't remember every wish I made
when I blew out my candles,
or every whispered hope at 11:11.
I don't remember each tear-soaked prayer
nor every plea I sent to angels,
carrying the weight of my grief.

But I remember the ache,
the heavy, unrelenting misery
that clung to my chest like a storm.
I remember the desperation that swallowed me whole,
when every breath felt like a cry for mercy,
and every heartbeat begged for a better life.

Today, I wake in the light of a wish fulfilled,
a prayer answered, a hope realised.
I may not remember every moment I longed for this,
but I will never forget the strength it took to keep hoping.

And I will always remember that even when the world feels still,
the universe tunes in to my every wish and will.

Caskets of the Past, Petals of the Future

I am a graveyard for every person I have ever been.
But around this graveyard,
there is a garden full of every person I am going to become.
The blooms grow around each casket of my past self,
a reminder that growth can bloom from every wound.

The graveyard is a tribute to my past,
but the garden is a toast to my future.

And my soul often lingers between the two,
sometimes mourning how things used to be,
sometimes celebrating what is yet to come.

Dawn After Dusk

I yearn to heal.

I don't just want to hush the shadows that cloud my thoughts,
because silence does not drown grief's howl.
And I'm not longing for merely a few good days,
for gloom always follows.

I seek a healing that mends my soul,
that rekindles the bliss I have forgotten.
A healing that takes root within me,
so my heart no longer sinks
when it is placed upon the ship of old wounds.

I covet the moment when darkness bids farewell;
I ache to finally welcome the dawn—
the dawn where my healing light resides.

Heartsease

There are times when you feel suffocated,
when the constant chatter wears on your nerves.
The grass in everyone else's garden appears greener than yours,
and suddenly, every success seems worthless.

There will be days, no matter how much you wash your face,
comb your hair, or spray yourself with soft scents of grace,
you won't be able to wash away the disgust within.
When everything you once loved feels like a chore to do,
you'll wish to peel your skin,
to rinse your body in hopes of feeling new.

Those are the days when nothing makes sense,
when no one's around, and you're left in suspense,
with only yourself to lean upon.

So don't chase after someone's unrequited love or praise;
you'll regret it when you're lost in a haze.
For only you can guide yourself through,
when everything seems to come unglued.

Everyone can leave, and everything can end,
but you will forever remain;
your heart and soul will be your closest friend.
That's not a curse, but a gift to hold,
for no one will love you as selflessly, as bold.

Believe me,
when you learn to love yourself like you do others,
you'll find in every part of you a reason to recover.

Don't think you're selfish—
believe you're loving someone selflessly yet again,
and for once, that someone is you.

The Blacksmith of Life

Time does not heal; it forges.
The ticking of the clock's hands does not make the pain fade away.
Rather, its steady pulse weaves sorrow deeper,
threading heartache into the fabric of the soul.

Time is a constant reminder that though the hours pass,
the wounds still sting,
raw beneath the surface.
But time is not the enemy; it is the blacksmith,
wielding its hammer to temper our spirit.

In the fires of loss, it shapes the soul,
turning grief into hardened armour.
And the scars that endure through time tell the story of survival,
of a heart that learned to mend the wreckage.

Time does not heal; it transforms,
moulding our broken pieces into resilience.

Anger's Last Breath

At some point,
you have to throw away that anger,
shed that sadness, and move on.
At some point,
you have to let go of the weight that anchors you down,

The flames of anger scorch no soul but your own;
the tides of sadness drown no one else but you.

Let anger dissipate like fog beneath the rising sun.
Seek the liberation that lies hidden beneath resentment's chains.
Forgive, not for their sake, but for yours.

Release the grip that tightens around your heart,
a constant reminder of the wounds that once consumed you,
and breathe deeply into the space where anger once thrived.

Autonomy

It's finally time to let go.
No longer do I wish to harbour a grudge,
or flip through our memories,
mourning the death of what we once had.

I'm setting my heart free,
liberating it from the cage of your shadow.
My soul craves to break through,
to reclaim the freedom it once knew.

So, I am letting you go, finally granting you forgiveness.
Not out of a desire to bring you back,
nor from lingering love,
but because my spirit deserves to find peace,
and I seek a solace that will never cease.

I have given enough control to your memories,
and I am ready to seize it back.
Because at last, it's time for me.
It's time to embrace the life that sets me free.

Thank You

Thank you for shattering my soul,
so I could gather every shard,
treating each fragment with warmth and care
that you never had the strength to share.

Thank you for ignoring all my sorrows,
so my heart could learn to fight its battles all alone.

Thank you for never loving me,
for pushing me toward the door,
so I could seek the warmth of arms
that truly know my worth and more.

You never gave me the fairytale I longed for,
but your lessons carved paths no requited love could weave.
Your absence was once a haunting void,
but now it's a garden where my spirit can breathe.

Sleepless Nights, Earned Days

People often laughed
when I sighed over a grade only slightly above average.
My classmates sneered in bitterness
when I argued with teachers over every mark I believed I deserved.
My concerns and fears were often dismissed,
because what do I have to lose?

But they did not see the sacrifices made,
the opportunities forgone, the prices paid.
The constant pressure to excel,
and the stories of failure that I am afraid to tell.
They are blind to the isolation that comes with the pursuit of perfection,
and the loneliness that accompanies ambition's direction.

But it has all been worth it.
Because it is not just about scraping by,
or seeing my paper plastered with a passing grade.

It is about knowing I had tried my best,
and the satisfaction of seeing those sleepless nights finally manifest.
It is about the constant effort to get everything right,
because I feel like I am incompetent otherwise.
It is about the pride that comes with the chase;
the feeling of knowing that wherever I am standing,
I have earned my place.

And when they tell me,
"Why're you worried? You'll pass anyway,"
I want to scream and tell them everything I have to say,
but I bite my tongue,
for my success will speak louder than them all one day.

The Art of Letting Go

Letting go is difficult.

Every time you move forward,
a lingering memory manages to hold you back.
Every joyous moment soon gives way to the ache of absence,
as if something vital is missing.

But to reclaim the freedom your soul deserves,
you must part with the ghosts that once felt like home.
Those walls that held you now bind your spirit,
and you must let them crumble, allow your heart to roam.

It's natural to grieve what has slipped away,
to acknowledge the pain of what cannot be.
But in that surrender, there lies a promise:
a chance to heal, to grow, to find your peace.

So, surrender to the ebb and flow,
and accept the silence where laughter once bloomed.
Trust that from this silence, a new song will find room.

The Best Friend in the Mirror

Everyone often shows pity when I tell them about my best friend,
but they haven't seen me like she has.
On my darkest days, she's the gentle hand that brushes through my hair,
the whisper that wipes away my tears.

She pushes me to be my best self
and reads my favourite books so I can live in a world better than reality.
She's the one who knows every flaw and every dream,
who celebrates my wins and whispers through my doubts.

Some may call it loneliness,
but in truth, I've found a treasure in this bond.
After all, she is the first breath I drew in this life,
and she'll be the heartbeat I carry into the next.

Dear Me,

I'm sorry.
I'm sorry for giving them every piece of you,
for treating you like my worst enemy,
and for every word I have uttered against you.

I promise I will make you a priority—
give you the love you have always deserved.
I will offer you the importance I once sought from others.
In the end, it's only you and me.

No more neglect, no more disregard;
I will care for you as I should have all along.
You are my first home,
and I am finally ready to come back.

Starlit Reverie

I want to run and run until there is nothing but the stars in sight,
to leave behind these places that hold my past so tight,
for they leave my soul parched for respite.
I yearn for the city lights to fade,
for the noise to go away.

Under the vast canvas of the endless cosmic sea,
I'll chase the constellations, let my spirit roam free.
And in the tranquil darkness, I will find my peace;
perhaps in the realm of stardust, I will finally be free.

I want to run and run, where the universe expands,
to find my piece of heaven in those distant lands.
For it's there, among the stars, that I'll finally be at ease.

CHAPTER 5

For Words of Comfort

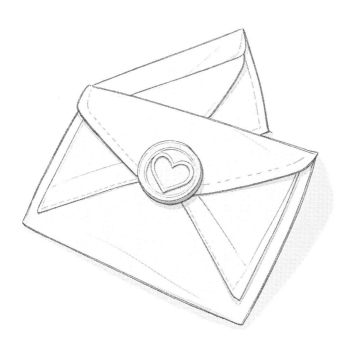

Equanimity

You deserve to be cherished,
flowers in hand, doors opened wide.
You deserve to feel loved even on your darkest days,
a hand to hold when nothing feels right.

But your worth is not measured by the absence of these joys.
You do not deserve to have a tear-stained face
while your heart yearns for love.
Don't let doubt erode the shores of your soul.

You are worthy of every joy this world can give,
of moments that lift you, reminding you to live.

Breathe in the promise that tomorrow will bring;
let time weave its thread, for patience is life's greatest gift.

Seeking Salvation

It's okay to crave the comfort of gentle hands,
to embrace your vulnerability.
It's okay to let someone else be your guide,
because even strength sometimes needs a place to confide.

A plant, strong and self-sufficient, standing tall,
still reaches for the rain to fall.
Despite its independence and its roots so deep,
it draws life from nature's love and grace.

So, it's okay to yearn for warmth and care,
to seek the sun in skies once bare.
On this path of life, we don't walk alone,
for the journey entirely without others would be far too monotone.

Love Awaits

When your heart aches,
when you start to build walls again,
and when you find yourself shattered, questioning every piece,
it's okay to feel adrift.

I promise, there are still souls out there,
eager to find their home in yours.

There are hearts that will dream of you,
filling the empty spaces with a love that overflows.
They will hold open doors and
embrace every inch of you that has been left coarse.

And when the weight of your scars feels too heavy,
know there are arms strong enough to bear it.
They'll wrap you close, like sunlight on the skin,
warming the spaces where cold once crept in.

Love waits patiently, like dawn's soft glow,
ready to lift you through every low.
It will seep through the cracks where pain once thrived,
growing new strength where hope survives.

The Path to Serenity

You will heal from all the things that rot in your heart.
The lump in your throat will cease.
The anxiety in your stomach will be washed over by serenity.

You will find moments of stillness,
where the chaos quiets and your breath becomes a balm.
In those fleeting seconds,
you will realise the weight you carry is not all you are.

You will grow roots in the soil of your own heart,
nurtured by strength, patience, and time.
And when the storms come, as they sometimes do,
you will stand firm, knowing the rain nourishes your spirit.

So trust in the process, in the gentle unfolding,
for healing is not linear; it's a journey of its own.
Each day, a step closer to the wholeness you seek,
each moment a reminder that you are beautifully alive.

Another Day

Some days, you will sit in your car,
wondering what to do with your life.
On another day, you will use the same car
to drive to your favourite place.

Some days, the sky won't be blue enough,
wearing a cloak of grey.
On another day, it will be the bluest hue you've ever seen.

Some days, you will feel worthless.
On another day,
you'll hear something that reminds you otherwise.

So, don't slip away in the shadow of 'some days.'
Stay a little longer to find your way.
Stay for the possibility that tomorrow will be better.

Maybe not the tomorrow after today,
but the tomorrow after *some* day.

Caught in the Web of Time

You can wish for a gentler past,
for when laughter echoed in familiar halls.
You can mourn the moments that slipped away,
each feeling a weight that settles deep.
You can spend your life praying you did things right,
but if every moment slips by, you'll lose track of light.

You will keep longing for change,
oblivious to when the stars will align.
But life will not wait,
it will go on, moments passing in a blur.
The dreams you held close,
the joys left behind, will all be caught in the trap of passed time.

The regret will dawn when it is too late;
the desperation will ache
when you can no longer chase the moments you let slip away.

Monotone Stories

Stop telling yourself that when something falls apart,
you must simply let it go as if life demands a swift farewell.
Sure, life will march on, with or without your consent,
but that doesn't mean your heart should move to its relentless rhythm.

You needn't build walls around every emotion,
forcing yourself to bottle them up like secrets.
Even the strongest vessels crack under pressure.

You are not merely the main character in this tale;
you are the narrator, shaping every chapter.

So take a breath—there's no audience waiting for your next act;
you control the pace of your growth, your feelings.
What's the fun in a monotone story anyway?

Just Enough

If a light is too bright,
perhaps it is the room that's small.
In spacious realms,
the light will shine just right.
If you are "too much,"
perhaps it's because they are not enough.

For those who only know the depths of night,
your radiance will be their guiding light.
When you lie beneath the starry sky together,
the glow of stars will fade away
in the presence of your luminous shine.

Stay

There are still so many sunsets to catch,
roads yet to wander, and tastes you've never met.
So stay.
Not for some grand, elusive purpose—
but for the gentle breeze that touches your skin,
the quiet rhythm of the stream,
the soft embrace of your blanket.

And when you question life's purpose,
take a look in the mirror, into your own eyes;
you'll find the answer waiting in that quiet gaze.

Stay for your dreams,
the sparks that light you up,
for the moments where you've truly lived.
Stay,
because life, in all its small wonders,
is still waiting for you.

CHAPTER 6

For the Path to Growing Up

Waves of Fate

You can spend your whole life charting every corner and bend,
mapping out the peaks and valleys,
plotting the course through every storm,
but you will never foresee the sudden gusts
that change the tide beneath your sails.
The tempests of change
will laugh at all your maps and compass points,
shattering your illusions.

Lost in the chaos,
your meticulously drawn lines
will be drowned by the roaring waves of fate.
Each carefully laid plan will be torn apart,
leaving you adrift in a sea of uncertainty.

You may cling to the fragments of your shattered dreams,
struggling to navigate a world unbound by your designs.
But in the relentless storm,
no anchor will hold,
no safe harbour will wait—
only the ceaseless, uncaring sea.

And when you are swallowed by the dark, unyielding night,
you will realise the fragility of control.

Too Young

You tell me I'm too young to understand,
too young to carry the weight of the world.
Yet here I stand, with your burdens in hand,
while my dreams lie dormant, unfurled.

Am I no longer young
when you place your baggage on my shoulders?
Does my youth simply disappear
when you leave my face stained in tears?
You wrap me in worries that aren't even mine,
as if the clock of my youth has suddenly frayed.

It seems as if the child in me only comes alive when it suits your needs,
then fades away, lost and forgotten,
as you shatter its innocence into fragments.

Time's Tapestry

Time is a thief.
It slipped through my fingers like the sand from my first sandcastle.
It snuck away when my grandmother would gently swing me to sleep.
It ran with my first best friend to hide in a corner far away from me.

But time is a reminder too.
It dances in the photos I keep.
It swings by when my father sits and tells me stories.
It lives in parts of me,
every second stolen piling up to a skyscraper of memories.

Maybe time is just hungry for the love we share;
maybe it steals our souvenirs to live vicariously.
I stop to think yet again, and it has me wondering…
Is time really a thief?

The Stain of Yesterday

Some days, I am soaring above life's vast sea,
living the way I never dreamed possible.
The past seems like a distant shore,
fading like a sunset swallowed by night.
What once was a hurricane now stirs only ripples.

But then come other days—
when shadows fall like heavy curtains,
a fragment of what used to be slips into view.
A word, or sight,
and I am pulled back into a spiral down a worn-out path.
It is on those days that emptiness settles in,
where my heart should be,
there is only a hollow ache.

I know the past is meant to be left behind,
so why do its echoes linger in my mind?
Why does its mark cling to my heart like a stain,
casting a shadow over joy, whispering ballads of pain?

Nostalgia's Grip

I look at the empty walls in my bedroom a lot more these days;
there are still marks on them from the posters I used to have up.

I linger for hours in front of my closet,
not lost in choices,
but burdened by the weight of what lies ahead—
the day I'll pack this wardrobe into a suitcase
and journey to a place that feels like a distant dream.

One day, I won't return to this room after long school days,
and the sound of bickering with my brother will fade into silence.
I'm not afraid of growing up;
rather, I shudder at the thought of my childhood memories
turning into a hazy fog.

It's not the act of growing up that frightens me,
but the bittersweet farewell to everything I once held dear,
for it is in the echoes of laughter and the warmth of yesterday
that my heart finds peace.

Farewell to Familiarity

I know I wanted this.
I know it's all part of life.
But why do my hands shake
as I load the trunk of my father's car?

Is it the fear of starting a new chapter,
or the shame of leaving behind the role I have played for years?

I cannot grow if I am caged within this box;
I cannot open my wings and soar
if the sky here is only as high as the ceiling.

So why does my heart ache on the plane?
Why do my arms want to chase my father's embrace?
Why does my mouth long for my mother's meals?

The apprehension tugs at my soul, but its solution is at home,
and I am leaving home; I am leaving without solace.

I am leaving without emotional refuge,
hoping the whispers of my dreams can overpower
the screams of my guilt.

The Gift of Youth

I love being young.
I love laughing over stupid inside jokes
and sharing my beloved delicacies with my closest girls.

I love sinking my teeth into my favourite meal
and screaming the lyrics to my go-to songs with a racing heart.
It is a gift, this stage of life.

It may not be perfect,
because in these years,
I will lose a lot and gain even more.
I will make a million mistakes and shed tears.
Every day will not be a bundle of joy;
some will be filled with anger,
and others with pure sadness.

But the rollercoaster of my youth is the simplest one that life has to offer.
Even if the people I cherish now become mere memories in ten years,
they will exist in the part of my brain that is the happiest.
For we shared the most vulnerable and carefree moments of our lives;
we shared our youth.

The Weight of Return

I want to go home.
But I don't know if
home will embrace me with loving hands.

Will they remember me for who I was,
or hate me for who I have become?
Will home bring me solace,
or will it reopen the wounds I ran away from?

The Flight of Memories

The flight of time reserves countless seats for nostalgia.
I sit right beside it, gazing out from the windows.
Below, there is a mosaic of experiences, vibrant and serene.

As the plane prepares for landing,
a new chapter is in sight,
with newer journeys and destinations calling my name.

But the shadows loom, heavy with my plight.

In the distance, the past calls softly,
a whisper of laughter, now tinged with pain.
As the clouds drift by, I search for solace,
yet memories linger like a haunting refrain.

I wonder if the sky will ever forget
the colours of my joy, painted bright and bold.
Will it carry my stories in its embrace?

The heartache of fleeting moments is one that grows
until my heart is sour with longing's woes.

The Ferris Wheel

At 2 years old, I owned a small, sepia Ferris wheel.
It was brought to my house only a little before I was—
a welcoming gift.

Each porcelain seat was dressed with pink flowers,
housing little bears with smiles so bright.
I often gazed at it, dreaming of the hours
when my father would take me to a real Ferris wheel,
seating me close to the glass, taking flight.

At 8 years old, I climbed on my first Ferris wheel.
My heart raced with fear; heights made me uneasy.
I floated high above, with a dizzying feel.
My feet longed the cement walkway below,
where the ground felt solid and my worries would flee.

At 15 years old,
I neither own a toy Ferris wheel,
nor do I recall the last time I sat on a real one.

It's ironic.

When I had a tiny wheel,
I was lost in dreams of something grander,
too consumed by longing to embrace its gentle spin.
When I finally rode the big wheel,
I threw tantrums in the clouds,
blinded to the beauty that danced below.

Now, with neither in sight,
all I want is to find joy in things as simple as
miniature bears on a Ferris wheel.
All I wish is to be that high in the sky again—
away from the harsh lines of these weary roads
and the cacophony of voices that haunt my days.

Not So Sweet Sixteen

When I turned 10,
all I could dream about was my thirteenth birthday,
the year I'd finally be a teenager
and do all the cool things the 8th graders could do.

Yet when I turned 13,
nothing truly changed.
I still felt like a wanderer in a vast forest,
having explored only a fraction of its secrets.

I imagined that at 16,
I'd step into a high school movie,
celebrating a grand sweet sixteen,
with a crowd big enough to fill a ballroom.

Now, as I stand on the brink of 16,
the sweetest age, or so they say,
I find I no longer crave a spotlight,
or wish for all eyes to rest on me.

The persistent urge to appeal to everyone has burnt out.
The only thing that matters now is not how much I know about this world,
or how similar my life is to those coming-of-age movies,
but rather how I spend this bittersweet age and
the lessons I unravel on every new page.

The Dance of Growth

Growing up is letting go over and over again
like shedding your layers, trading them for new skin.
But there's no manual to guide you through the shifting tides,
no map to navigate the heart's tangled roads.

Your parents, once guardians through all your strife,
take a step back, their embrace now a distant echo of home.

Your best friends, once just a call away, scatter far and wide,
each shared secret now a whisper in the wind.
The laughter amidst high school maths class sits heavy in the air,
an aching reminder of moments that once felt like forever.

Growing up is the dance duet between letting go and holding on,
a fragile balance where the past intertwines with the present's swift stride.

CHAPTER 7

For the Echoes of Love

Glimpse of Home

In a sky full of stars,
in a garden brimming with blooms of every hue,
in a candy shop stocked with sweet-filled jars,
the only treasure my eyes wander around looking for is you.
For in your embrace, my heart finds its room,

To Papa, My Guiding Star

I tried to write a poem about my father and failed.
My pen never stopped; the poem never ended.
Was I supposed to write about his selfless love?
Or should I have confined my words to the feeling of his warmth?

In every attempt, his presence overflowed the page.
Too vast for lines to contain, too deep for words to convey.
Should I have captured his laughter,
a sound that will forever be my favourite,
or the strength of his shoulders,
carrying every burden of mine?

With gentle hands, he grew the gardens of my dreams,
nurturing seeds of hope in life's ever-changing streams.
His belief in my wings, even when I feared the heights,
gave me the courage to soar through the darkest nights.

For every word I write, a hundred remain unsaid;
in the silence of my verses, his boundless love spreads.
No poem can capture his essence,
for he's more than words or lines could ever meet.

Yet here I write,
knowing words will never suffice to paint the portrait of my father,
the man to whom I owe not just this world,
but the universe of my gratitude and love.

The Rhythm of Us

We follow from rhythm to rhythm, a sight of pure grace.
The world seems a blur
as if there is no one but us,
no one but our hearts moving at a perfect pace.

The stars are our witnesses, the moon our spotlight
as we twirl behind the kitchen counter.
Love is our music,
replacing every other melody that once echoed among these walls.

With this dance, I find our souls intertwined and our fate aligned.
At this moment, I'd rather be nowhere else, with no one else.
I'd want nothing else to think, nothing else to feel, nothing else to see.

In this moment,
I have everything.

When Souls Fit

Words lost, found, and lost again,
my pen scrawls and scratches in search of the perfect words.
This is not just any piece; this piece is about my best friend.
A friendship that's always been beyond
the norm, beyond the simple give-and-take,
beyond the clichés of childhood fate.

I always moved from place to place,
so a childhood best friend was never in my cards.
I simply made friends along the way
and moved on from that bond to build the next one.

But there has always been something different about this friendship;
it was the kind I struggled to replace.
We shared our laughter and our tears, every secret and every fear,
the kind of pair everyone knew was inseparable,
through every friend group and every fight.

Her name echoes through my home
as if she's part of it all and I'm never alone.
And even though our thoughts don't always fit like parts of a puzzle,
our souls certainly do.
No matter the bitter days and misunderstandings,
she will always be the girl I count on,
the girl I share my heaviest burdens with,
the girl who's always there to celebrate.

If I am blessed with any more lives,
I hope she is my best friend in them all.

Seasons of You

You are my soft blanket in winter's embrace,
an icy popsicle against summer's fierce blaze.

In every garden, I search for your favourite blooms,
and in every soul, I listen for your soothing tunes.

My pillows, once soaked with silent tears,
held the echoes of heartache through countless years.

But since your arrival, a light has unfurled.
These pillows now cradle my joy,
and the walls, once silent, now dance with my light,
whispering stories of love in the night.

Unbound Energy

"Energy can neither be created nor destroyed."
One of the basic principles of physics,
rather stupid in your opinion.
You never understood where all the energy would go,
or where it came from if it could not be created.

I thought you were only being immature,
but it all makes sense now.

Because I have all this love for you,
all this energy that flows,
but I do not know where it came from, and
I do not know where this love will go.

Mirror, Mirror

The three of us look into a mirror,
hoping our makeup's nearly perfect.
Compliments fill the room
as our laughter overtakes any other noise.

Sunlight peeks through the room;
it yearns to catch a glimpse of this moment—
a moment I'd like to freeze.

In the mirror's reflection,
I see love.
Love that knows no conditions,
that feels like a warm embrace,
that forever exists.

And in each other's company,
we've found where we belong.
In each other's company,
we've found an unparalleled bond.

The Light of My Dreams

میرے خوابوں کی روشنی

اندھیرے میں چمک جائیں، میرا دل تو صرف تیری روشنی اور
چاہے سورج آسمان میں چھا جائے، یا ستارے بھی
اس حسین مسکراہٹ کی تلاش میں ہی مر جائے

Whether the sun shines in the sky, or the stars shine in the darkness, my heart simply dies in the search for only your light and that gorgeous smile.

chaahe suraj aasmaan mein cha jaaye, ya sitare bhi andhere mein chamak jaaye, mera dil toh sirf teri roshni aur iss haseen muskurahat ki talaash mein hi mar jaaye.

Rife with You

You were handed the worst parts of me,
yet you cradled them with the utmost fragility.

For every meltdown,
your hand found mine.
For every burst of anger,
your soothing voice brought me solace.
Even from miles apart,
I felt your gentle embrace linger in the air.

The words I spoke began to mirror yours,
and your favourite colour was one I searched for in everything.
Dark chocolate was once my worst nightmare,
but it tasted sweeter with you by my side.
And those love songs I once detested,
they started to weave your name into their verses.

Whether it's the worst or the best parts of me,
you exist within them all,
and there's nothing more fascinating yet frightening than that.

Enamoured

I love the glint of joy in your eyes
at the sight of dogs,
the way your fingers dance when you attempt to weave a lie.
I love the way you never pull away first from a hug,
and the sound of your laughter
that follows my worst jokes.

I love your apologies,
always wrapped in a pinky promise—
a vow to never let anger linger,
to keep our hearts intertwined.

I could spend endless years
writing down all the reasons I admire you,
but even a universe of words would fall short,
unable to capture the depth of my love.
Nothing could explain this feeling,
not even the lords of love themselves.

Acknowledgments

As you turn the pages of this journey, I want to acknowledge the gratitude that flows like an endless river, carrying the echoes of those who have shaped my story. This book would not have been possible without the inspiration, support, and love of many people and things.

Firstly, thank you to my angels above, my paternal grandparents, *my Baba and Amma,* who are not here to see my dreams turn into reality. Though we are universes apart, your pride and love shine through in every accomplishment I hold dear. Even without hearing your words of pride, the warmth you've left in my heart will always remind me of your love.

On the same note, thank you to my maternal grandparents, *my Nana and Nani*. I cherish the summers spent with you, filled with memories that instilled in me the values I hold today. Thank you for the secret ice cream treats; you hold a part of my heart that is incredibly dear to me.

Moving on, I'd like to thank the man who has truly made this, and every aspiration of mine possible. Thank you, papa, my silent cheerleader. The rock of our family, whose unwavering support and encouragement have been the wind beneath my wings. Your trust in me has been a constant source of strength, and I am forever grateful for the sacrifices you've made for me to pursue my dreams. I love you more than words can express.

Thank you to the hands that brew my favourite coffee, whose tough love and resilience have shaped me into the person I am today. Mumma, your lessons have prepared me to face life's challenges head-on, and I am stronger because of it. I cherish the memories of our late-night talks, our laughter, and our tears.

Thank you to my brother, for teaching me the wizardry of Google Docs so I could write this book without drowning in paper. You've been my silent supporter and the keeper of my secrets. I'm incredibly proud of the person you've become and grateful for your unwavering support. Thanks for being my personal IT department and for letting me proofread your work (it made for good practice). I promise to keep using these writing skills to help you with your homework assignments (maybe not *all* the answers, though). Thank you for everything.

Of course, any page dedicated to gratitude would be incomplete without acknowledging my friends, who have walked with me through the darkest nights and the brightest days.

A special acknowledgment to:

Natasha, who answered all the midnight calls, wrapping me in comfort and pulling me back to light.

Faria, who embraced every rough draft of my work and the corner of my soul, seeing beauty in my chaos.

Eliza, my favourite source of warm hugs and unwavering cheerleader, always reminding me of my worth.

Devanshi, who welcomed all my ramblings with compassion, guiding me through my darkest moments.

You four have seen the mess behind the metaphors – thank you for loving me through it all.

Thank you to my teachers. Ms. Mais, your guidance ignited a fire that still burns bright. Ms Lydia, who saw the spark in me, even when I couldn't see it myself, and Ms. Manuella, your encouragement gave me the courage to share my words with the world.

I can't forget to acknowledge my trusty headphones, my escape from the chaos: You've carried my secrets and played the songs that comfort me when I need it most. In the lyrics of Noah Kahan and the melodies of Phoebe Bridgers, I found the soundtrack to my healing and creation. You've been with me through sleepless nights and rough mornings, offering a bit of calm when everything else felt too much.

Thank you to every heart that's shared its story with me, unknowingly planting seeds for these verses—your experiences have become the soil in which my words flourish.

And the biggest acknowledgment to the version of me who refused to break. The girl who found rhythm in heartbeats and rhyme in goodbyes.

You transformed your wounds into windows, letting light pour onto these pages. This book is your victory song.

Thank you to everyone who has contributed to this journey, whether through words, actions, or simply being present. This book is a testament to the power of that community, love, and resilience.

About the Author

Eisha Dileep is an author who writes to make sense of the world around her. Born in Pakistan and now living in Dubai, she draws inspiration from the places she's been and the people she's met. Her poems explore themes of nostalgia, change, and the hidden layers of everyday life. Through her writing, she hopes to capture fleeting moments and give voice to emotions we all share but rarely express. When she isn't writing, she enjoys capturing the world through her camera and working on crafts, always drawn to the creative process in its many forms.

Made in the USA
Columbia, SC
03 November 2024